CRYPTONAIRE

Getting Started with the Biggest "Millionaire Maker" Asset: A Complete Guide

PARKER COLE

Contents

INTRODUCTION

If you still have questions about cryptocurrencies, you're not alone. A Huobi report estimates that nearly 30% of American adults possess cryptocurrency. In contrast, 40% of respondents claim to have "not much awareness" or "no knowledge" of the digital form of money.

So even cryptocurrency investors are in the dark.

This book is intended to provide you with a better understanding of cryptocurrencies and how to conduct market research if you decide to make an investment.

CHAPTER 1
HISTORY OF CRYPTOCURRENCY

When David Chaum, an American cryptographer, published a conference paper explaining an early type of anonymous cryptographic electronic money in 1983, the concept of cryptocurrencies first came to light. The idea was to create a kind of money that could be distributed anonymously and without the need for centralized organizations (i.e., banks). Based on his original concepts, Chaum created the proto-cryptocurrency Digicash in 1995. Before money could be delivered to a destination, it needed certain encryption keys and used software to withdraw money from a bank.

In 1998, Nick Szabo invented Bit Gold, which is frequently seen as Bitcoin's immediate forerunner. It demanded that participants devote computer resources to deciphering cryptographic puzzles, and those who succeeded were rewarded. When combined with Chaum's work, it produces a system that closely resembles Bitcoin.

However, without the aid of a centralized authority, Szabo was unable to resolve the famed double-spending issue (digital data can be copied and pasted). As a result, it took another ten years before an unknown individual or group acting under the alias Satoshi Nakamoto launched the development of Bitcoin and other cryptocurrencies by disseminating a white paper titled "Bitcoin - A Peer to Peer Electronic Cash System."

BITCOIN AS THE FIRST CRYPTO

The Bitcoin white paper outlining the operation of the Bitcoin blockchain network was released on October 31, 2008, by Satoshi Nakamoto. When Satoshi bought Bitcoin.org on August 18, 2008, they formally started working on the bitcoin project. Although it's not the focus of this article, it's important to note that blockchain technology, which at its most basic level is constructing immutable data structures, is essential to the existence of Bitcoin (and all other cryptocurrencies).

The tale of Bitcoin was beginning. On January 3, 2009, the Bitcoin network's initial block was mined by Satoshi Nakamoto. They included a headline from The Times in this first block as a permanent allusion to the economic circumstances—which included bank bailouts and a centralized financial system—that Bitcoin was in part a reaction to.

EVOLUTION OF THE ALTCOIN.

Altcoin is known as 'other coin apart from Bitcoin". Bitcoin was demonstrating its real-world value even if it didn't yet have much of a value. It reached a high of $1.06 in February 2011 before falling back to about 87 cents. The price shot up in the spring, partially as a result of a Forbes article on the brand-new "cryptocurrency." Bitcoin's price increased from 86 cents to $8.89 between early April and the end of May. The price of the currency more than tripled in a week to roughly $27 on June 1, following the publication *by Gawker of an article about its attractiveness in the online drug trafficking community. The market value of all bitcoins in use was close to $130 million. But by September 2011, the price had reverted to about $4.77.*

One of many forks (i.e., updated versions) of Bitcoin that debuted in October of that same year was Litecoin. With PPCoin, Namecoin, and ten other cryptocurrencies trailing in the background in the earliest CoinMarketCap database (from May 2013), Litecoin quickly overtook them as the second-largest cryptocurrency by market cap. These cryptocurrencies, some of which split off from Bitcoin and others based on new code, were rapidly termed "altcoins."

Bitcoin values increased substantially throughout 2012, and the Bitcoin Foundation was created in September of that year to support the growth and adoption of Bitcoin. Ripple, at the time known as OpenCoin, was also introduced that year, and the project later attracted venture funding. In 2013, the price of bitcoin fluctuated wildly due to a variety of legal, criminal, regulatory, and software-related challenges. Its price peaked at $755 on November 19 before plummeting to $378 the next day. On November 30, it had risen all the way to $1,163. But this was the start of another long-term decline that culminated in Bitcoin falling down to $152 by January 2015.

CHAPTER 2

UNDERSTANDING BLOCK AND HOW IT WORKS.

Blockchain is an information-recording technology that makes it difficult or impossible to alter, hack, or cheat the system. Essentially, a blockchain is a network of computer systems that duplicates and distributes a digital log of transactions.

Blockchain aims to enable the distribution and recording of digital information without its editing. So, a blockchain serves as the basis for immutable ledgers or records of transactions that cannot be changed, removed, or destroyed.

EXAMPLES OF BLOCKCHAIN.

Blockchains are often used in instances like Bitcoin and Ethereum. Anyone can connect to the blockchain and conduct transactions on them.

However, there are many other Blockchain Networks including;

- *Stellar.*
- *XDC Network.*
- *Tezos*
- *Hyperledger Fabric.*
- *Hyperledger sawstooth*
- *Hedera hashgraph*
- *Ripple*
- *Quorum*

The Bitcoin blockchain is undoubtedly the most well-known because it represents roughly 40% of the value of all cryptocurrencies.

CHAPTER 3

INTRODUCTION TO CRYPTO TRADING

Trading cryptocurrencies involves making predictions about their future price movements or purchasing and selling the underlying coins on an exchange.

BUYING AND SELLING CRYPTO VIA AN EXCHANGE

Purchasing bitcoins through an exchange entails buying the actual coins. To open a position on an exchange, you must deposit the whole asset value, open an exchange account, and keep the cryptocurrency tokens in your own wallet until you are ready to sell them.

Exchanges have a very steep learning curve since you have to master the technology and understand how to interpret the data. The amount you may deposit on several exchanges is likewise restricted, and keeping an account can be highly expensive.

HOW CRYPTO MARKET WORKS

The marketplaces for cryptocurrencies are decentralized, which implies that no single entity, like a government, issues or supports them. They move through a network of computers instead. Cryptocurrencies can, however, be purchased, sold, and held in "wallets" as well as on exchanges.

In contrast to conventional currencies, cryptocurrencies only exist as a shared, blockchain-stored record of ownership. A user *sends cryptocurrency units to another user's digital wallet when they desire to send them to that person. The transaction isn't deemed complete until it has been mined, validated, and uploaded to the blockchain. New cryptocurrency tokens are often created in the same manner.*

CHAPTER 4

WHAT DO YOU NEED TO INVEST IN CRYPTOCURRENCY?

Although the concept of cryptocurrencies can be intimidating to novice investors, there aren't many requirements to get started. To begin, all you have to do investing in cryptocurrencies are:

1. Secure internet connection

2. *Personal identification documents*

3. *Bank account information*

All done! A stockbroker is another option for buying cryptocurrencies. Most of your personal and financial data will already be on file in this situation.

WHAT IS CRYPTO EXCHANGE?

A platform for trading cryptocurrencies is referred to as a cryptocurrency exchange. Despite the fact that exchanges frequently offer minimal costs, their more complicated user interfaces, numerous trading kinds, and sophisticated performance charts might be confusing to novice cryptocurrency investors.

The most well-known cryptocurrency exchanges are Binance.US, Coinbase, and Gemini. Although the conventional trading interfaces of these organizations may be intimidating to novices, especially those without an experience in trading stocks, they also provide simple, user-friendly purchase options.

HOW TO BUY CRYPTOCURRENCY.

Selecting a broker or cryptocurrency exchange is the first step in purchasing cryptocurrency.

By providing user-friendly interfaces that communicate with exchanges on your behalf, cryptocurrency brokers simplify the process of buying cryptocurrencies. Some impose costs that are higher than exchanges. Others make the promise to be "free" while profiting by either failing to execute your trade at the best available market price or selling information about what you and other traders are buying and selling to *huge brokerages or funds. SoFi and Robinhood are two of the best-known bitcoin dealers.*

Although brokers are undoubtedly practical, you should exercise caution because you could be unable to remove your bitcoin holdings from the platform. For instance, you cannot withdraw your cryptocurrency holdings through Robinhood or SoFi. Even while it might not seem like a big deal, savvy cryptocurrency investors prefer to store their money in digital wallets for added security. For even greater security, some people opt for offline, hardware cryptocurrency wallets.

Create an Account and Verify It. *You can register to open an account after selecting a bitcoin broker or exchange. You might need to prove your identification, depending on the platform* and how much you intend to purchase. To avoid fraud and adhere to federal regulations, this is a crucial step.

Until the verification procedure is finished, you might not be able to buy or trade cryptocurrencies. You might be required to post a selfie to the platform to demonstrate that your appearance matches the documentation you submit, along with a copy of your passport or driver's license.

Deposit Cash to Invest. You must make sure you have money in your account in order to purchase cryptocurrency. By connecting your bank account, approving a wire transfer, or even making a purchase with a debit or credit card, you can add *money to your cryptocurrency account. You might need to wait a couple of days before using the funds you deposit to purchase cryptocurrencies, depending on the exchange or broker and your payment method.*

While certain exchanges or brokers permit credit card deposits, doing so is exceedingly risky—and costly. Companies that handle credit cards see bitcoin purchases made with them as cash advances. In addition to having to pay additional cash advance fees, this also means that they are liable to greater interest rates than conventional purchases. For instance, when you make a cash advance, you can be required to pay 5% of the transaction amount. Additionally, any expenses your cryptocurrency exchange or brokerage may impose might total up to 5% on their own, meaning you could lose 10% of your cryptocurrency purchase to fees.

Place your order*. You are prepared to place your first crypto order after funds have been deposited into your account. Choose from hundreds of cryptocurrencies, from well-known ones like Bitcoin and Ethereum to less well-known ones.*

You can specify a cryptocurrency's ticker symbol (Bitcoin's is BTC, for example) and the desired number of coins when choosing which cryptocurrency to buy. You may buy fractional shares of cryptocurrencies from the majority of exchanges and brokers, enabling you to purchase a small portion of expensive tokens like Bitcoin or Ethereum that would otherwise cost thousands to hold.

Choose a storage method. Because they are not covered by insurance like the Federal Deposit Insurance Corp. (FDIC), cryptocurrency exchanges are vulnerable to theft and hacking. As millions of dollars' worth of Bitcoin have already been lost due to forgetting or misplacing the codes to access your account, you might potentially lose your investment. Because of this, having a secure location to keep your cryptocurrency is crucial.

As mentioned above, you can have little to no control over how your bitcoin is stored if you purchase it through a broker. You have more choices if you buy cryptocurrencies on an exchange like maintaining the cryptocurrency on the exchange.

When you purchase bitcoin, it is often kept in an exchange-affiliated "crypto wallet." You could relocate it away from the exchange to a different hot or cold wallet if you don't like the provider your exchange partners with or if you want to store it somewhere more safe. You might have to fork up a little money to achieve this, depending on the exchange and the quantity of your transfer.

HOT/COLD WALLET.

Hot wallet. *These are online-stored cryptocurrency wallets that may be used on tablets, PCs, phones, or other internet-connected devices. Hot wallets are useful, but since they are* *still linked to the internet, there is a greater chance of theft.*

Cold wallet*. Cold crypto wallets are your most safe alternative for storing cryptocurrency because they aren't online. They appear as external gadgets like hard drives or USB drives. Cold wallets require caution, though, since you could never be able to retrieve your bitcoin if you lose the keycode associated with them or the device malfunctions. While the same could occur with certain hot wallets, others are managed by custodians who, In the case of a lockout, can assist you in regaining access to your account.*

CHAPTER 5
AVOIDING CRYPTO SCAM.

1. *Be wary of any offers or prizes you see on social media. Because screenshots can be faked and manipulated, you shouldn't rely on them in reply messages.*

2. *Never send cryptocurrency to giveaways in order to verify your address.*

3. *Search for any company contacting you via social media using your preferred search engine. The offer is probably untrue if it seems too good to be true.*

4. *Be wary of "get-rich-quick" scams. The urge to seize a chance to get wealthy quickly can*

And finally, always research before investing. It's crucial to research cryptocurrency exchanges before investing your time and money in them because new coin varieties are always emerging. This entails asking questions about exchanges you've never heard of before and even checking to see if they've ever been linked to complaints or scams.

Examine the degree to which exchanges are open about their liquidity and ICO policies; this is a sign of a trustworthy business. It might even entail contacting the exchange personally and inquiring. It's also important to confirm whether an exchange makes use of blockchain technology, which enhances transaction security.

PROTECTING YOURSELF WHILE INVESTING IN CRYPTO.

Securing a wallet is one of the finest ways to safeguard your investment. Hardware "cold storage" or "cold wallet" devices are the most secure choice between the two. These wallets serve as a tangible repository for tokens or money and have a USB drive-like appearance.

For cryptocurrency lovers, a hardware wallet is the safest choice, but because of its inconvenience, an account with a reputable exchange might be a secure and practical choice for holding your cryptocurrency if you simply intend to invest in and hold a handful of well-known coins.

WHAT AFFECTS CRYPTOCURRENCY.

One of the most important elements influencing cryptocurrency prices is investor sentiment, which is influenced by a mix of supply, demand, manufacturing costs, competition, regulatory developments, and the ensuing media coverage.

Availability on exchanges, Governance and Regulations are also factors that determines its price.

How does cryptocurrency lose value?

The cost of trading in cryptocurrencies is influenced by the crypto monetary system, just as it is by the popularity of a company's products. A cryptocurrency's value is primarily impacted by its supply, market demand, accessibility, and rival cryptocurrencies.

CONCLUTION.

For small enterprises, cryptocurrencies work great. You can receive money from anywhere in the world by setting up an address, which eliminates the burden of dealing with paperwork, rules from the government, and bank costs.

Cryptocurrency may be a wise investment if you're ready to acknowledge that it's a high-risk bet that could pay off but that there's also a substantial chance you could lose everything. In 2022, a global cryptocurrency price crash caused the price of cryptocurrencies, including bitcoin, to decrease. However, economists predict that by 2030, the global cryptocurrency market will have increased by more than threefold.

CONCLUSION